ENERGY SOURCES
Facts · Issues · The Future

WATER POWER

NEIL MORRIS

A+
Smart Apple Media

Published by Smart Apple Media
2140 Howard Drive West
North Mankato, MN 56003
Designed by Guy Callaby
Edited by Mary-Jane Wilkins
Artwork by Graham Rosewarne
Picture research by Su Alexander

Photograph acknowledgements
Title page James Davis; Eye Ubiquitous/Corbis; page 4 ESA/PLI/Corbis;
5 Dave G. Houser/Corbis; 6 Terry Jennings; 7 Elio Ciol/Corbis;
8 Bettmann/Corbis; 9 Graham Howden; Cordaiy Photo Library Ltd/
Corbis; 11t Charles E. Rotkin/Corbis, b Judyth Platt; Ecoscene/Corbis;
13 Lester Lefkowitz/Corbis; 14 Carl & Ann Purcell/Corbis; 15t James
Davis; Eye Ubiquitous/Corbis, b xinhua/Xinhua/Corbis; Liz Bates/17
Practical Action; 18 Yann Arthus-Bertrand/Corbis; 19 Courtesy of Nova
Scotia Power Inc; 20 Jaimie Taylor; 21 Courtesy of Ocean Power
Delivery Ltd; 23t Ralph White/Corbis, b Natural Energy Laboratory of
Hawaii Authority, State of Hawaii; 24 Christopher J. Morris/Corbis; 25
Wild Country/Corbis; 26 Collart Herve/Corbis Sygma; 27t Collart
Herve/Corbis Sygma, b Paul Marshall/Wildfowl & Wetlands Trust; 29
Chrinch Gryniewicz; Ecoscene/Corbis; Front cover Philip James
Corwin/Corbis

Printed in China

Library of Congress Cataloging-in-Publication Data

Morris, Neil, 1946-
Water power / by Neil Morris.
p. cm. — (Energy sources)
ISBN-13: 978-1-58340-909-1
1. Water power—Juvenile literature. I. Title.

TC146.M67 2006
333.91'4—dc22   2006003242

First Edition

9 8 7 6 5 4 3 2 1

Contents

The world of water

The world's water is a valuable source of energy. We use it to provide the power to operate machines, as well as to light and heat our homes, offices, and factories.

From space, Earth looks mainly blue and white. The blue is the water of the oceans and seas that cover more than two-thirds of the surface. The white swirls are clouds.

The term "energy" comes from the Greek word *energos*, meaning "active" or "working." Energy sources help other things become active and do work, such as lifting or moving objects. For example, water power can be used to make electricity. When you switch on a light, the energy to make it light up might have come from the power of moving water.

Never-ending cycle

Our world of water moves continuously in a never-ending cycle, powered by the energy of the sun. As the sun heats Earth's oceans, water changes into a gas (called water vapor) and rises into the air. There it cools and forms tiny droplets of water that join together to make clouds. Eventually, the water falls back to Earth as rain, and on land much of it comes together to form rivers, which take the water back to the ocean. There the water cycle starts all over again, providing us with a renewable resource.

The famous Niagara Falls, on the United States-Canada border, show the dramatic power of falling water. At the falls, some water is diverted through tunnels to produce electricity.

Going with the flow

When you put your hand in a fast-flowing stream or under a running faucet, you can feel the power of running water. Rivers flow naturally as water moves from higher to lower ground by the force of gravity. Water in the oceans also moves by the natural power of wind, currents, and tides. We can use all of these different forms of moving water as a source of energy to produce mechanical and electrical power.

Early waterwheels

We don't know exactly when people first started using water power to drive mills and grind grain into flour. The first watermills may have been built at Alexandria, in Egypt, nearly 2,500 years ago.

The idea of watermills spread throughout the ancient Roman empire, replacing hand-driven grindstones, which were less efficient and much harder to work. In 11th-century Britain, the Domesday Book survey counted more than 5,000 watermills in the country.

In later centuries, waterwheels were used to drive bellows, mechanical hammers, and looms for making textiles. For all of these uses, the wheel was fitted with paddles that were pushed by the water to make it turn. An undershot wheel was turned by water flowing at its base. In the overshot design, water poured over the top of the wheel.

Many waterwheels had a special channel, called a race, that carried water from a nearby river or stream.

Raising water

Different systems of waterwheels have been used since ancient times to raise water from rivers. The main use was to irrigate the surrounding countryside. For the famous Hanging Gardens of Babylon, which made up one of the Seven Wonders of the Ancient World, the water was raised from the Euphrates River. The Babylonians probably used human or animal power.

On the Orontes River, in modern Syria, giant wheels called norias used the river's flow to raise water for irrigation. The water was lifted to the top of a tower and then channeled to nearby towns and fields.

Flour mills

The ancient Romans were famous for their water technology. They built aqueducts to carry water from rivers and other sources to many of their cities. They also used water to power mills. The ruins of one amazing example have been found near Arles, in southern France. There an aqueduct brought water to the top of a hill, where it flowed down past eight pairs of overshot wheels, turning one after the other. The 16 wheels drove millstones that ground enough grain to feed the 12,000 people of Arles.

The giant wooden norias at Hama, on the Orontes River, are 65 feet (20 m) across. The oldest surviving wheel dates from the 15th century, and they were first built hundreds of years earlier.

Steam engines

During the 18th century, the Industrial Revolution introduced completely new methods of producing goods. The revolution was powered by steam, produced by boiling water. The world's first steam engine had been invented 1,700 years earlier by a Greek mathematician called Hero of Alexandria. This was not a very practical machine, but in 1785, Scottish engineer James Watt improved on earlier steam engines.

New steam-driven machinery made it possible to produce huge amounts of textiles in large factories. Steam was also used to power trains and ships, changing the world of transportation forever. Unlike earlier water power, other energy sources were needed to heat the water and turn it into steam. Coal was the most popular fuel, and it is still used to produce steam—and electricity—in coal-fired power plants today.

In this original Watt engine, steam pushed a piston up and down. This was connected to a rod, which turned a large wheel.

Horsepower

In 1769, British inventor Richard Arkwright developed a water-powered spinning machine that he called a water frame. In the same year, James Watt took out a patent to protect the invention of his steam engine. This was an improved version of an earlier invention by Thomas Newcomen, and it was soon installed in some of Britain's largest factories. These included flour mills, printing presses, and breweries. Watt compared his engines' work rate to that of horses and so invented the unit of measurement called "horsepower." Later scientists devised a new unit of energy and called it a "watt" after the inventor.

From Rocket to Mallard

Steam power also ushered in the age of railroads. This began in 1804, when the first steam locomotive pulled wagons along rails in an iron factory. Twenty-six years later, a steam locomotive called the *Rocket* pulled a special train to open the Liverpool and Manchester Railway. This new locomotive, which was designed and built by George Stephenson and his son Robert, had a top speed of 29 miles (47 km) per hour. Steam locomotives became faster and more efficient until they were replaced by diesel power in the mid-20th century.

The streamlined Mallard *was the fastest steam locomotive ever built. In 1938, it achieved a world record steam train speed of 126 miles (203 km) per hour.*

Rivers, dams, and reservoirs

Rivers have been used as a source of electrical power since the end of the 19th century. The power is harnessed by building a dam across the river, creating a reservoir behind it. The water is allowed to rush through a specially built channel, where it turns the blades of a turbine—a bit like an earlier waterwheel. The turbine drives a generator, which produces electricity.

The first water-powered plant was built on the Fox River in Wisconsin in 1882. It was used to power electric trams along the streets of a nearby town. Since then, dams have become much bigger and are used to provide power for whole communities. Today, about a fifth of the world's electricity is generated this way. Electricity that is produced by water is called hydroelectricity.

A hydroelectric dam has a channel called a penstock through which water flows from the reservoir to make electricity. After turning a turbine, the water flows on down the river.

turbine

penstock

Using the reservoir

The reservoir behind a dam ensures that there is always a large supply of water ready for use. The flow of water into the penstock can be controlled so that just the right amount flows to the turbines. The reservoir is useful in times of drought, when the river is low. But if there are floods and too much water, spillways can be opened to let it flow through the dam and on down the river. The reservoir can also be used for irrigating crops and supplying water to towns.

Pumped storage

Pumped-storage plants are different from hydroelectric dams, because they store and use the same supply of water over and over again. They are made up of two reservoirs, or lakes, one much higher than the other. When electricity is needed during times of high demand, water is allowed to flow down from the upper reservoir and turn turbines before being collected in the lower reservoir. When demand is low, water is pumped back up to the higher reservoir using electricity from the system.

The large reservoir behind the 3,500-foot-wide (1055 m) Shasta Dam, on the Sacramento River in California. The reservoir, called Shasta Lake, has a shoreline nearly 370 miles (600 km) long. It is home to sturgeon, trout, and bass and is popular with fishermen.

The dam and upper reservoir of the Ffestiniog pumped-storage plant in Britain. From here, water falls more than 1,000 feet (300 m) through tunnels in the mountain to four turbines.

Turbines and generators

In 1831, British scientist Michael Faraday discovered that he could create electricity by moving a magnet through a coil of copper wire. This led to the invention of the electric generator.

The generator works by changing mechanical energy into electrical energy. In a hydroelectric dam, the power of moving water provides mechanical energy by hitting the blades of a turbine and turning them. The blades are connected to a shaft that is attached to a generator. Inside the generator, the shaft makes magnets spin inside wire coils to produce electricity. In dams, both turbines and generators are huge pieces of equipment. The generator is housed in a building above the level of the water, where it can be checked and serviced by engineers.

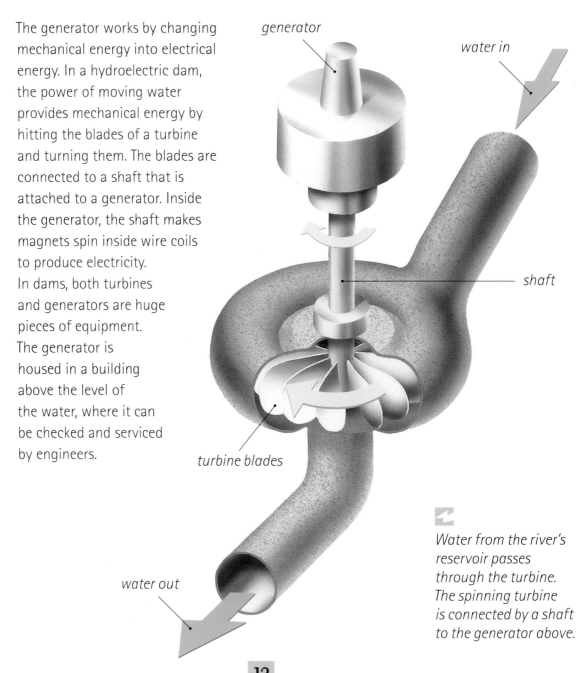

generator

water in

shaft

turbine blades

water out

Water from the river's reservoir passes through the turbine. The spinning turbine is connected by a shaft to the generator above.

Generating more power

Hydroelectric dams usually have several penstocks, through which the water flows, and a number of generators. This allows each dam to produce a huge amount of electricity. The famous Hoover Dam, on the Arizona-Nevada border, has 4 penstocks and 17 generators.

Powering cities

Electricity generated at a power plant is changed and made more powerful by devices called transformers. This makes it easier to carry the electric current long distances along power lines. The lines are carried on tall pylons to towns and cities, where another set of transformers changes the current back to a lower voltage (or power). Then the electricity can be sent to homes and factories.

THE WEIGHT OF WATER

The Hoover Dam's reservoir, called Lake Mead, is 590 feet (180 m) deep. When it was first created and filled in 1936, the weight of the water caused earth tremors in the area. No damage was done, and engineers learned from this to allow reservoirs to fill more slowly.

Some of the generators at the Hoover Dam. Each one can supply enough electricity for 100,000 homes. The engineer in the foreground offers a sense of the vast size of each generator.

From Aswan to Three Gorges

There are large, powerful rivers on all continents of the world, and in recent years, hydroelectric dams have become bigger and more powerful.

Dams produce vast amounts of electricity. In 1971, the Aswan High Dam was completed on the world's longest river, the Nile, in Egypt. This created a vast reservoir, called Lake Nasser, which is more than 300 miles (500 km) long. The huge dam is more than 2.2 miles (3.6 km) wide. It is made of earth and granite, with a core of clay and cement. Its 12 generators produced half of Egypt's electricity when the power plant opened, making it possible to provide electricity to many villages for the first time.

Power cables lead away from the Aswan High Dam, which can generate up to 2,100 megawatts of electricity.

Power across borders

In 1991, the world's most powerful dam began making electricity on the upper part of the Paraná, the second-longest river in South America (after the Amazon). The concrete dam is called Itaipú, meaning "the stone that sings," and it lies on a part of the river that forms the border between Brazil and Paraguay. The dam's 18 generators produce 12,600 megawatts of electricity, which provide a quarter of Brazil's needs and more than three-quarters of Paraguay's.

The large spillway next to the Itaipú dam has 14 sluice gates that control the flow of the river, especially in times of flood.

The completed Three Gorges Dam will be 600 feet (185 m) high and more than 1.2 miles (2 km) wide. It is being built for flood control as well as to provide electricity.

LOST HOMES

People opposed to the Three Gorges Dam point out that up to two million people will have to move from their homes because of the flooding caused by the huge reservoir behind the dam. The reservoir will flood 19 cities and more than 300 villages.

Electricity from the Chang Jiang

When it is completed in 2009, the Three Gorges Dam in China will generate more electricity than any other. Its 26 generators will produce 18,200 megawatts. Building work on this huge project started in 1993, adding another dam to those that already exist on the Chang Jiang, which is China's longest river. Power will be sent along transmission lines to eastern and central China, where it will bring electricity to millions of villagers for the first time.

Micro-hydro systems

Hydroelectric power can be produced on a small scale. In recent years, micro-hydro systems have become popular with people or small communities who want to produce their own electricity.

Some of the turbines used are much smaller than earlier waterwheels, and the modern versions are designed to work with low water speed. They can power generators that provide electricity for lights, heating, tools, pumps, and many other machines. One of the great advantages is that electricity can be produced very close to where it is used. This means there is no need for expensive pylons and heavy transmission lines, and so the systems have very little effect on the environment.

Micro-hydro systems are just like small-scale versions of hydroelectric dams, but without a reservoir.

generator

In this Kenyan community, villagers have dug a channel from a fast-flowing river. Water flows down the channel to a small turbine and generator.

Replacing mains power

Micro systems can also replace mains power. In parts of southwest England, farmers have built their own hydro systems on streams that flow through their land. In many cases, the micro-hydro system replaces an existing old watermill. Some farmers have found this method so successful that at times they produce more electricity than they need. They sell the extra power by supplying it to the national grid, the network of power lines that supplies electricity to most homes.

REPLACING FOSSIL FUELS

Small-scale systems are very useful in small communities in developing countries, especially if they have no other source of electricity, or only expensive and polluting fossil fuels. In some parts of Kenya, in East Africa, micro-hydro systems are used on small streams. These help villagers who would otherwise have to use kerosene lamps for lighting.

Tidal barrages

The oceans' tides are another powerful source of natural energy. People realized this hundreds of years ago, and wooden tidal mills were built at river mouths and estuaries in England and France.

Wooden gates were closed at high tide, and when the tide turned, the water flowed out through millwheels, which were used to turn millstones and grind corn. More recently, large barrages have been built across wide estuaries. They work in a similar way to hydroelectric dams, with the river estuary acting like a reservoir. The outgoing tide (and in some cases the incoming tide, too) flows through tunnels that contain turbines connected to electric generators. Many tidal barrages have been planned and designed, but few have been built. This is because of high costs and concerns about the effects they may have on coastal environments.

The Rance barrage stretches 1,080 feet (330 m) across an estuary. It has a lock (in the foreground) so boats can pass along the estuary.

Ebb and flow

The barrage on the Rance River, in northern France, became the world's first working tidal power plant in 1966. Its 24 turbines produce 240 megawatts of electricity—about a quarter as much as a coal-fired power plant (and less than 1/50th as much as the Itaipú dam). The turbines are turned by both incoming and outgoing tides, but, like most tidal barrages, they work better when the tide is going out from the river to the sea.

Spring and neap tides

The pull from the gravity of the moon and the sun causes Earth's tides. The force of gravity pulls a bulge of water toward the moon, creating a high tide on that part of Earth. As Earth spins and the moon revolves around it, the bulge of water moves and the tides go in and out at a particular place. When the moon and sun are in line with each other, the pull of gravity is greater and there are higher, spring tides. But when the sun and moon are at right angles to Earth, they produce lower, neap tides. Tidal barrages are best located in regions where the tidal range (the difference between high and low tide) is great.

The Annapolis tidal generating station has been operating in the Bay of Fundy, on the Canadian coast, since 1984. This region has some of the world's biggest tidal ranges—up to 48 feet (14.5 m) between high and low tides.

MAINTAINING A BALANCE

Tidal barrages run the risk of upsetting the delicate balance of estuary ecosystems by allowing the build-up of sediment. This could affect the wild birds and animals that live on the local wetlands and mudflats by changing their habitat.

Using wave energy

Waves are caused by wind blowing over the surface of the ocean. They are another form of moving water, and they too can be used to produce electricity.

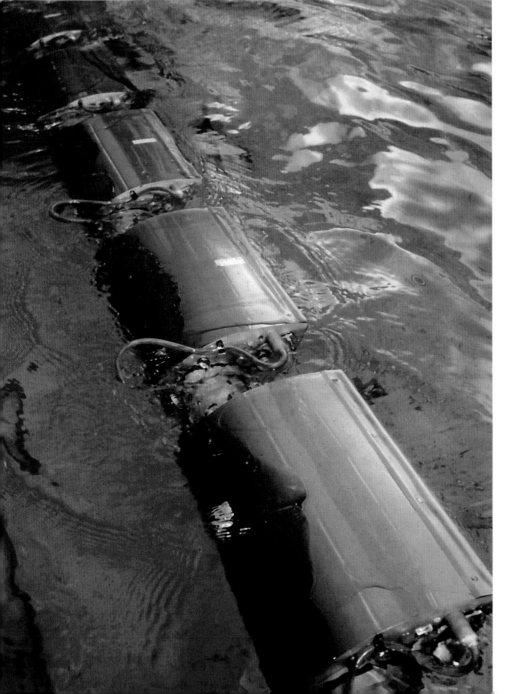

Some wave generators float on the sea, with hinged parts that bob up and down with the waves. The up-and-down movement turns a central shaft that is connected to a turbine. These devices, called nodding ducks, are efficient, but they are dependent on sea conditions. One day of calm—and very little power production—might be followed by a storm with giant waves, which could break or sink the ducks. Scientists are working on these problems, and many believe that wave generators have enormous potential for the future.

A row of nodding ducks is really a series of hinged flaps that move up and down with the waves.

On the shore

Engineers have been designing shore-based wave stations for 20 years. Most have been built on rocky coasts, where waves crash against the shore. The most common type is called an oscillating water-column (or OWC) generator. This works by allowing the breaking waves to push water up through a concrete column or metal pipe. The rising water acts like a piston, pushing air ahead of it, and the moving air turns the blades of a turbine.

Power of a sea snake

The Pelamis wave-energy machine is named after a sea snake, because that's what it looks like. About 400 feet (120 m) long and 11 feet (3.5 m) wide, this jointed "snake" lies half-submerged on the surface of the ocean, where waves move its hinged joints. This movement powers hydraulic motors that drive electric generators. The electricity flows down a cable to the seabed, and from there to land. Several machines together could make a wave farm.

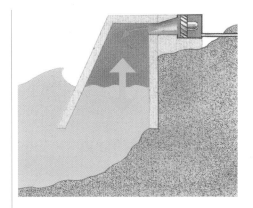

Diagram of an OWC generator. This kind of wave generator has to be very strong, otherwise it could be destroyed or damaged in a storm.

The Pelamis wave-energy machine. A wave farm of these sea snakes covering one square mile (2.6 sq km) of ocean would provide enough electricity for 52,000 homes.

Ocean thermal devices

In the tropical oceans of the world, there is a difference of about 36 °F (20°C) between the temperature of the warm surface and the cold depths.

Scientists realized they could use the temperature difference to generate electricity. They designed various devices using a system called Ocean Thermal Energy Conversion (OTEC), which works like a regrigerator in reverse. Warm surface seawater is pumped through a heat exchanger, where a refrigeration fluid boils and turns to vapor. The expanding vapor drives a turbine. Cold water is pumped from the depths to cool the vapor and turn it back into a liquid, which then goes through the system again. The turbine drives a generator, and the resulting electricity is sent to shore along an underwater cable.

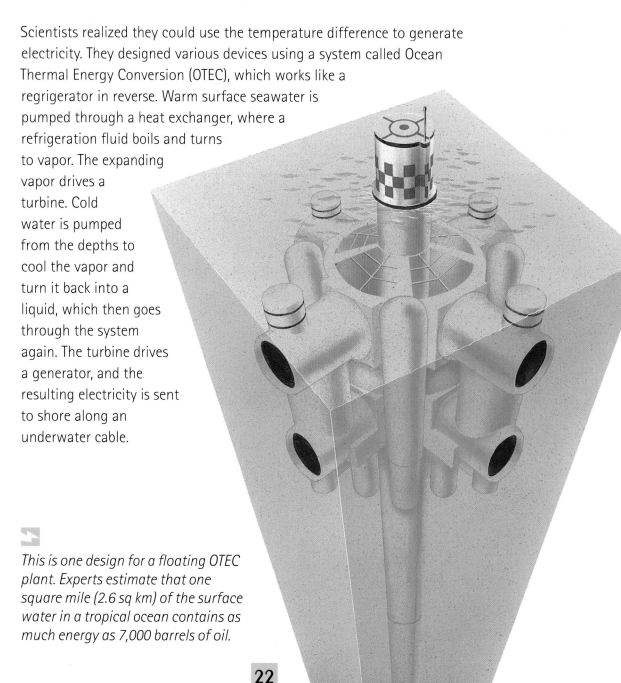

This is one design for a floating OTEC plant. Experts estimate that one square mile (2.6 sq km) of the surface water in a tropical ocean contains as much energy as 7,000 barrels of oil.

Stored heat

The world's oceans collect and store heat energy from the sun. Their water heats up more slowly than the land, but it cools down more slowly, too. Near the equator, the surface temperature can rise to 86 °F (30 °C). The warm surface waters go down to a depth of about 490 feet (150 m) and below that level, the temperature drops rapidly to about 41 °F (5 °C). Below about 3,300 feet (1,000 m), the ocean is completely dark all the time, and close to the deep-sea floor, the temperature ranges between 34 and 39 °F (1–4 °C)

Scientists use small research submarines to learn more about the world's oceans. Researchers hope to find new ways to use water power.

Continuing research

A French physicist named Jacques Arsène d'Arsonval was the first to suggest tapping the thermal energy of the ocean, in 1881. Today, research on this is carried out all over the world. The world's tropical islands are useful locations, and the generated electricity could provide power for island communities. Research began in Hawaii in the 1970s, and in 1979, a converted U.S. navy barge moored 1.2 miles (2 km) offshore was producing electricity by the OTEC method. Since then, Hawaiian scientists have also successfully tested land-based systems.

An experimental OTEC plant in Hawaii. It uses water from a depth of 2,000 feet (600 m), where it has a temperature of just 43 °F (6 °C).

Around the world

Earth's water is spread around the planet—in oceans, seas, lakes, rivers, and streams—so it can be used everywhere as an energy source.

Hydroelectric dams on rivers produce far more electricity than waves, tides, or other water sources. Nearly a third of the world's hydropower is produced in Europe, and about a quarter in Asia. North America produces slightly less but has the world's two largest producing countries—Canada and the U.S. They are followed by Brazil and China. All of these countries have major mountain ranges and big rivers, which help in the production of hydroelectricity. But this energy source is useful in smaller, developing countries too, where micro-hydro systems are becoming more important.

USING ENERGY

Both Norway and Nepal produce most of their electricity by hydropower. The great difference between them is that Nepal is much poorer and uses far less electricity. On average, a Norwegian uses as much electricity every day as more than 400 Nepalese people.

The Montreal skyline is lit up by electricity at dusk. More than half of Canada's electricity comes from water power.

Norwegian hydropower

Norway is a mountainous country with heavy rainfall and many rivers and waterfalls. This makes it an ideal region for producing hydroelectricity. Altogether, there are about 850 hydroelectric power plants in the country, and they produce nearly all of the electricity the country needs.

As a result, Norway can export much of the oil that it recovers near its North Sea coast. When the oil runs out, the rivers will still be flowing to provide power. Norway also has rough seas along its coast, and scientists are testing fixed wave generators in some places.

Nepalese farmers grow rice on terraced fields in the Himalayan foothills. Some farmers are installing micro-hydro turbines in the irrigation channels that flow down the hillsides to produce electricity.

In the Himalayas

The kingdom of Nepal lies high in the Himalayan mountains. The country has no coastline, and its greatest natural resources are its forests and rivers, which flow south into India. As in Norway, almost all of Nepal's electricity is produced by hydropower.

Benefits and problems

As a renewable energy source, water has many advantages over nonrenewable sources such as fossil fuels. Exploiting water power is less damaging to the environment, and its supply is guaranteed.

For these reasons, many countries have been trying to increase their use of water power in recent years. Environmentalists point out, however, that dams and barrages can also have a damaging effect. It has recently been discovered, for example, that large reservoirs give off gases such as carbon dioxide and methane. These gases contribute to the greenhouse effect. The governments of individual countries have to weigh the advantages and disadvantages of new water-power systems.

The Tucurui Dam, on the Tocantins River in Brazil. This river flows 1,680 miles (2,700 km) to the delta of the Amazon. It has many natural rapids and waterfalls, as well as man-made dams.

DROWNED FORESTS

Dam reservoirs drown huge areas of land. In Brazil, environmentalists are trying to stop more large dams from being built. The Tucurui dam's reservoir flooded a large area of the Amazon rain forest, and 30,000 people were forced to move. Some people say this is the price of progress, but much of the dam's electricity is used to power aluminum plants rather than to help local people.

Changing coasts

Changing the natural flow of water can have huge effects on coastal regions. Since the 1980s, there have been proposals to build a tidal barrage across the estuary of the Severn River, between southwest England and Wales. Experts believe this would be a good site for electricity generation, although the construction would be very expensive. More importantly for environmentalists, the barrage would almost certainly upset the delicate balance of the estuary. If the barrage allows sediment to build up, this could have a dramatic effect on the local wetlands and mudflats, which are important for wildlife.

One small part of the brazil-nut forest drowned by the Tucurui reservoir. More than 925 square miles (2,400 square km) of forest were lost.

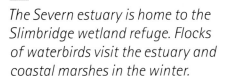

The Severn estuary is home to the Slimbridge wetland refuge. Flocks of waterbirds visit the estuary and coastal marshes in the winter.

27

Future trends

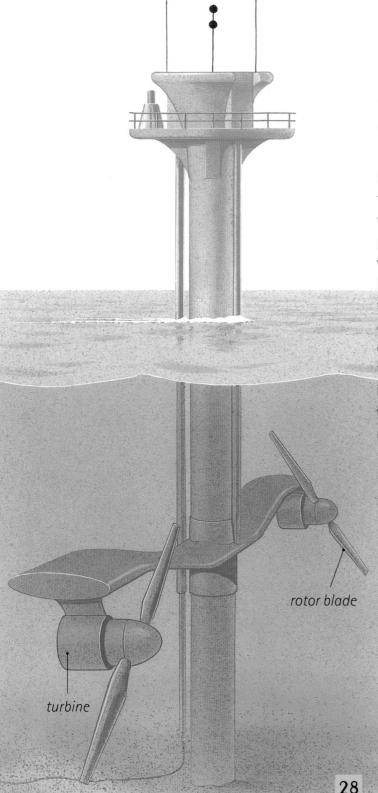

Renewable sources of energy will become even more important in the future, as the world's demand for energy and electricity continues to increase.

Early in the 21st century, scientists estimated that wave turbines could provide 1/10th of the world's energy. But demand for electricity is predicted to almost double over the next 25 years. In China, demand is growing even faster. Projects such as the huge Three Gorges Dam will provide much more power, but will this be enough? Most scientists believe that the power of currents, tides, and waves must be added to that of rivers, so that water power will grow in importance as fossil fuels run out. Perhaps new ways will also be found to use water to power machines, as it did centuries ago in watermills.

rotor blade

turbine

This artist's impression shows a design for a marine current turbine. It works like a submerged windmill, with the current acting like the wind and turning the twin rotor blades.

28

Capturing currents

As well as tides, ocean currents can be used to provide power. Currents are often strongest in narrow straits between islands and around headlands near the coast. Many different kinds of turbines are being developed. Some are floating devices, and others are fixed to the seabed in places where the water is not too deep. The movement of the currents turns the rotor blades of a turbine attached to a generator.

Tidal lagoons

Many experts believe that large dams and tidal barrages will be replaced by tidal lagoons. The idea is to build a sea wall of rock and rubble around the shallow waters of a coastal bay. Turbines are built into the wall at regular intervals, and these are turned when the tide comes in and goes out. Environmentalists believe that the bays would be less affected than estuaries by barrages. There are test projects in Britain, China, and elsewhere. Scientists have estimated that 25 tidal lagoons could generate a quarter of Britain's electricity.

Swansea Bay, in Wales, is one of the locations chosen for studying new technology. The tidal lagoon there would cover more than 2.7 square miles (7 sq km) of sea.

 # Glossary

aqueduct   A channel built to carry water.

bellows   A device that blows out air when squeezed.

coal-fired   Driven by the burning of coal.

current   A flow of water or electricity.

diesel   A fuel obtained from crude oil that is similar to gasoline.

environmentalist   A person who is concerned about and acts to protect the natural environment.

estuary   The wide mouth of a river where it meets the sea.

fossil fuel   A fuel (such as coal, oil, or natural gas) that comes from the remains of prehistoric plants and animals.

generator   A machine that turns mechanical energy into electrical energy.

gravity   The force that pulls an object toward the center of Earth or another planet.

greenhouse effect   The warming of Earth's surface (called global warming) caused largely by pollution from burning fossil fuels.

headland   A narrow piece of land jutting out from a coast into the sea.

hydroelectricity   Electricity produced by moving water, especially from a dam across a river.

hydropower   Electricity generated using water power.

Industrial Revolution   The rapid development of machinery, factories, and industry that began in the late 18th century.

irrigate   To water (land) in order to help crops grow.

kerosene   A fuel oil similar to gasoline.

lagoon   A coastal stretch of shallow water that is sometimes cut off from the sea.

loom   A device for weaving thread into cloth.